THIS BOOK BELONGS TO

The Library of

....

....

Thank you for Purchasing my book and taking the time to read it from front to back. I am always grateful when a reader chooses my work and I hope you enjoyed it!

With the vast selection available online, I am touched that you chose to be purchasing my work and take valuable time out of your life to read it. My hope is that you feel you made the right decision.

I very much would like to know what you thought of the book. Please take the time to write an honest and informative review on Amazon.com. Your experience and opinions will be of great benefit to me and those readers looking to make an informed choice.

With much thanks.

Table of Contents

SUMMARY

What is Macramé Knots and Patterns?: Macramé Knots and Patterns refer to a traditional craft technique that involves creating intricate patterns and designs using various types of knots. It is a form of textile art that dates back centuries and has gained popularity in recent years due to its versatility and aesthetic appeal.

Macramé knots are the building blocks of this craft, and there are numerous types of knots that can be used to create different patterns and textures. Some common knots include the square knot, half hitch knot, double half hitch knot, and the lark's head knot. Each knot has its own unique characteristics and can be combined in various ways to achieve different effects.

The patterns in macramé can range from simple and straightforward designs to more complex and intricate creations. Beginners often start with basic patterns such as wall hangings, plant hangers, or keychains, which involve using a few simple knots to create a decorative piece. As one gains more experience and skill, they can progress to more advanced patterns that involve multiple knots and techniques.

Macramé patterns can be created using a variety of materials, including cotton cord, jute, hemp, or even yarn. The choice of material can greatly impact the final look and feel of the piece. Thicker cords create a more substantial and chunky appearance, while thinner cords result in a more delicate and intricate design.

One of the appealing aspects of macramé is its versatility. It can be used to create a wide range of items, including home decor, accessories, and even clothing. Macramé wall hangings have become particularly popular in recent years, adding a bohemian and natural touch to any space. Macramé plant hangers are also widely used, allowing individuals to display their favorite plants in a unique and stylish way.

Learning macramé knots and patterns can be done through various resources, including books, online tutorials, and workshops. Many craft stores also offer macramé kits that include all the necessary materials and instructions to create a specific project. With practice and patience, anyone can master the art of macramé and create beautiful and personalized pieces.

In conclusion, macramé knots and patterns are a traditional craft technique that involves creating intricate designs using various types of knots. It is a versatile and creative art form that allows individuals to express their creativity and create unique pieces of decor and accessories. Whether you are a beginner or an experienced crafter, macramé offers endless possibilities for creating beautiful and personalized items.

Engaging with the Art and Craft of Macramé Knotting: Engaging with the art and craft of macramé knotting is a truly rewarding and fulfilling experience. Macramé, a form of textile-making using knotting techniques, has a rich history that dates back centuries. It originated in the 13th century in the Arab world and spread to Europe during the Moorish conquests. Over time, macramé has evolved and adapted to different cultures and styles, making it a versatile and diverse art form.

One of the most appealing aspects of macramé knotting is its accessibility. Whether you are a beginner or an experienced crafter, macramé offers a wide range of projects suitable for all skill levels. From simple plant hangers and wall hangings to intricate jewelry and clothing, there is something for everyone to create and enjoy.

Engaging with macramé knotting allows you to tap into your creativity and express yourself through the medium of knots and cords. The process of creating macramé pieces is not only visually pleasing but also meditative and calming. As you focus on each knot and weave, you enter a state of flow, where time seems to stand still and your mind becomes fully immersed in the task at hand. This mindful practice can be a form of therapy, helping to reduce stress and anxiety while promoting a sense of relaxation and well-being.

Furthermore, macramé knotting offers a unique opportunity to connect with the past and preserve traditional craftsmanship. By learning and practicing macramé techniques, you become part of a long lineage of artisans who have passed down their knowledge and skills through generations. This connection to history and heritage adds depth and meaning to your macramé journey, making it more than just a hobby or craft.

Engaging with the art and craft of macramé knotting also opens up a world of possibilities for personalization and customization. With a wide variety of cords, colors, and patterns to choose from, you can create macramé pieces that reflect your own style and taste. Whether you prefer a bohemian, minimalist, or modern aesthetic, macramé can be adapted to suit any interior or fashion style. This versatility allows you to infuse your own personality and creativity into each project, making it truly unique and one-of-a-kind.

In conclusion, engaging with the art and craft of macramé knotting is a fulfilling and enriching experience. It offers a creative outlet, a form of therapy, a connection to history, and a means of personal expression.

Using This Guide to Embark on Your Macramé Journey: Embarking on your macramé journey can be an exciting and fulfilling experience. Whether you are a beginner or have some experience with this craft, using a guide can greatly enhance your learning and help you create beautiful macramé pieces.

One of the first steps in starting your macramé journey is to find a comprehensive guide that suits your needs. There are many resources available, including books, online tutorials, and workshops. It is important to choose a guide that is well-written, easy to understand, and provides clear instructions. Look for guides that include step-by-step tutorials, detailed diagrams, and helpful tips and tricks.

Once you have found a suitable guide, it is time to gather the necessary materials. Macramé requires a few basic supplies, including cord or rope, scissors, and a dowel or ring to hang your finished piece. The type of cord you choose will depend on the project you are working on, so it is important to consult your guide for recommendations. Additionally, you may want to invest in some additional tools, such as a macramé board or tapestry needle, to make your macramé journey even more enjoyable.

With your materials in hand, it is time to dive into the world of macramé. Start by familiarizing yourself with the basic knots used in this craft, such as the square knot, half hitch knot, and lark's head knot. Your guide should provide detailed instructions on how to create these knots, as well as variations and combinations to create different patterns and designs.

As you progress in your macramé journey, don't be afraid to experiment and try new techniques. Macramé is a versatile craft that allows for endless creativity. Your guide may introduce you to advanced knots, such as the double half hitch or Josephine knot, which can add complexity and beauty to your projects. Additionally, you may want to explore different materials, such as colored cords or beads, to add a unique touch to your macramé pieces.

Throughout your macramé journey, it is important to practice patience and perseverance. Like any craft, macramé requires time and effort to master. Don't be discouraged if your first few projects don't turn out exactly as you envisioned. Instead, view them as learning experiences and opportunities for growth. With each project, you will improve your skills and gain confidence in your abilities.

The History and Evolution of Macramé Crochet: Macramé crochet is a textile art form that has a rich history and has evolved over time to become a popular craft today. The origins of macramé can be traced back to ancient civilizations, where it was used to create decorative and functional items.

The exact origins of macramé are difficult to pinpoint, as it was practiced by various cultures around the world. However, it is believed to have originated in the Middle East, where it was used by sailors to create intricate knots and patterns on their ships. These knots were not only decorative but also served practical purposes, such as securing items and creating handles.

Macramé crochet gained popularity during the Victorian era in Europe, where it was used to create elaborate lace-like patterns. It was considered a highly skilled craft and was often used to create intricate designs on clothing, home decor, and accessories. During this time, macramé was primarily practiced by women as a form of leisure and self-expression.

In the 20th century, macramé crochet experienced a resurgence in popularity, particularly during the hippie movement of the 1960s and 1970s. Macramé was embraced by the counterculture as a way to create unique and bohemian-inspired pieces. It was often used to create wall hangings, plant hangers, and jewelry, reflecting the free-spirited and nature-inspired aesthetic of the time.

As the years went by, macramé crochet continued to evolve and adapt to changing trends and styles. Today, it is still a popular craft, with modern macramé artists incorporating new techniques and materials into their work. Macramé workshops and classes are widely available, allowing people of all skill levels to learn and practice this ancient art form.

One of the reasons for the enduring popularity of macramé crochet is its versatility. It can be used to create a wide range of items, from small accessories like earrings and keychains to large-scale installations and home decor pieces. The intricate knots and patterns of macramé add a unique and handmade touch to any space or outfit.

In conclusion, the history and evolution of macramé crochet is a testament to the enduring appeal of this ancient craft. From its origins in ancient civilizations to its resurgence during the Victorian era and its continued popularity today, macramé has proven to be a versatile and timeless art form. Whether you are a beginner or an experienced crafter, macramé crochet offers endless possibilities for creativity and self-expression.

Materials, Tools, and Workspace Setup of Macramé Knotting:
Macramé knotting is a popular craft that involves creating intricate patterns and designs using various types of cords and knots. To get started with macramé knotting, you will need a few essential materials, tools, and a well-organized workspace setup.

Firstly, let's discuss the materials required for macramé knotting. The primary material used in macramé is cord, which can be made from various fibers such as cotton, jute, hemp, or nylon. The choice of cord depends on the desired look and feel of the finished project. Thicker cords are ideal for creating bold and chunky designs, while thinner cords are suitable for delicate and intricate patterns. Additionally, you may also need beads, charms, or other decorative elements to enhance your macramé creations.

Next, let's move on to the tools needed for macramé knotting. The most basic tool required is a pair of sharp scissors for cutting the cords to the desired lengths. You will also need a measuring tape or ruler to ensure accurate measurements. Additionally, a clipboard or a macramé board can be useful for holding your work in place while you knot. Some macramé enthusiasts also use pins or clips to secure their cords during the knotting process.

Now, let's discuss the importance of a well-organized workspace setup for macramé knotting. Having a dedicated workspace will not only make your macramé projects more enjoyable but also help you stay organized and focused. Start by finding a flat surface, such as a table or a desk, where you can comfortably work on your projects. Make sure the surface is clean and free from any obstructions that may hinder your knotting process.

To keep your cords organized, consider using cord organizers or small containers to store them. This will prevent tangling and make it easier to find the right cord when you need it. Additionally, having a designated area for your tools, such as a small tray or a toolbox, will ensure that everything is within reach and easily accessible.

Lighting is another crucial aspect of your workspace setup. Ensure that you have adequate lighting to see your knots clearly and avoid any mistakes. Natural light is ideal, but if that's not possible, consider using a desk lamp or other suitable lighting options.

Lastly, it's essential to create a comfortable and ergonomic workspace. Macramé knotting can be a time-consuming activity, so investing in a comfortable chair with proper back support is highly recommended.

The Significance and Applications of Macramé: Macramé is a versatile and ancient art form that involves creating intricate patterns and designs by knotting various types of cords together. It has a rich history that dates back thousands of years and has been practiced by different cultures around the world. The word "macramé" is derived from the Arabic word "miqramah," which means "fringe".

One of the significant aspects of macramé is its versatility. It can be used to create a wide range of items, including wall hangings, plant hangers, jewelry, clothing, and even furniture. The possibilities are endless, and the only limit is one's imagination. Macramé allows individuals to express their creativity and create unique and personalized pieces that reflect their style and personality.

Macramé has also gained popularity in recent years due to its therapeutic benefits. The repetitive and rhythmic motions involved in knotting can be calming and meditative, providing a sense of relaxation and stress relief. Many people find macramé to be a form of mindfulness practice, allowing them to focus their attention on the present moment and engage in a soothing and creative activity.

In addition to its therapeutic benefits, macramé has practical applications as well. For example, macramé plant hangers are not only aesthetically pleasing but also functional, as they allow individuals to hang their plants and create a unique and stylish display. Macramé wall hangings can add texture and visual interest to any space, while macramé jewelry can be a fashionable and trendy accessory.

Furthermore, macramé can be a sustainable and eco-friendly art form. It can be created using various types of cords, including natural fibers such as cotton, hemp, and jute. By using these materials, individuals can reduce their environmental impact and contribute to a more sustainable lifestyle. Additionally, macramé allows for upcycling and repurposing of materials, as old t-shirts or fabric scraps can be transformed into beautiful macramé creations.

Macramé also holds cultural significance in many societies. It has been used by different cultures throughout history as a form of decoration, symbolism, and storytelling. For example, in some Native American tribes, macramé was used to create dreamcatchers, which were believed to protect individuals from bad dreams and negative energy. In other cultures, macramé was used to create ceremonial garments or as a way to pass down traditions and cultural heritage.

Fundamental Knots in Macramé: Macramé, an ancient art form that involves knotting cords to create intricate patterns, has gained popularity in recent years. Whether you're a beginner or an experienced crafter, understanding the fundamental knots in macramé is essential to creating beautiful and unique designs.

One of the most basic knots in macramé is the square knot. This knot is created by crossing two cords over each other and then passing the ends through the loop created. By repeating this process, you can create a series of square knots that form a decorative pattern. The square knot is versatile and can be used to create a variety of designs, from simple bracelets to complex wall hangings.

Another important knot in macramé is the half hitch knot. This knot is created by taking one cord and wrapping it around another cord, then pulling it through the loop created. The half hitch knot is often used to create fringe or tassels in macramé projects. By combining multiple half hitch knots, you can create intricate and textured designs.

The lark's head knot is another fundamental knot in macramé. This knot is created by folding a cord in half and passing the folded end through a loop or ring. By pulling the loose ends of the cord through the folded end, you can secure the knot. The lark's head knot is commonly used to attach cords to a dowel or other base in macramé projects.

The spiral knot, also known as the half knot spiral, is a more advanced knot in macramé. This knot is created by taking two cords and crossing them over each other, then passing the ends through the loop created. By repeating this process, you can create a spiral pattern that adds depth and dimension to your macramé designs.

In addition to these fundamental knots, there are many other knots and techniques that can be used in macramé. These include the double half hitch knot, the square knot sennit, and the Josephine knot, among others. Each knot and technique offers its own unique possibilities for creating intricate and beautiful macramé designs.

Understanding and mastering the fundamental knots in macramé is the first step towards creating stunning and personalized macramé projects. By practicing these knots and experimenting with different combinations and variations, you can develop your own unique style and create one-of-a-kind pieces that showcase your creativity and skill. So grab some cords, a dowel, and get ready to dive into the world of macramé!

Combining Knots to Create Textures of Macramé Knotting:
Macramé knotting is a versatile and intricate art form that involves the creation of beautiful and intricate patterns by combining various knots. The process of combining knots in macramé allows for the creation of unique and textured designs that can be used in a variety of applications, such as wall hangings, plant hangers, and jewelry.

One of the key aspects of macramé knotting is the ability to combine different types of knots to create interesting and visually appealing textures. There are numerous types of knots that can be used in macramé, including square knots, half knots, double half hitch knots, and lark's head knots, among others. Each knot has its own unique characteristics and can be combined in different ways to achieve different effects.

For example, combining square knots with half knots can create a dense and tightly woven texture, while combining double half hitch knots with lark's head knots can create a more open and airy texture. By experimenting with different combinations of knots, macramé artists can create a wide range of textures that add depth and visual interest to their designs.

In addition to combining different types of knots, macramé artists can also vary the size and spacing of the knots to create even more texture. By using larger knots or spacing them further apart, a more pronounced texture can be achieved. Conversely, using smaller knots or spacing them closer together can create a more delicate and intricate texture.

The process of combining knots to create textures in macramé requires both creativity and skill. Macramé artists must have a deep understanding of the different types of knots and how they can be combined to achieve different effects. They must also have a keen eye for design and be able to envision how different combinations of knots will look when woven together.

Overall, combining knots in macramé allows for the creation of unique and textured designs that are visually stunning. Whether it's a wall hanging, a plant hanger, or a piece of jewelry, the textures created through the combination of knots add depth and visual interest to any macramé creation. With endless possibilities for knot combinations and variations in size and spacing, macramé artists can truly let their creativity shine and create one-of-a-kind pieces that showcase the beauty and intricacy of this ancient art form.

Practice Projects: Simple Keychains and Bracelets of Macramé Crochet:

Macramé crochet is a versatile and creative craft that allows you to create beautiful and intricate designs using just a few basic knots. If you're new to macramé crochet or looking for some practice projects to improve your skills, making simple keychains and bracelets is a great place to start.

Keychains and bracelets are small and manageable projects that require minimal materials and time, making them perfect for beginners or those with limited crafting experience. They also serve as great gifts or personal accessories, allowing you to showcase your creativity and style.

To get started, you'll need a few basic supplies. These include macramé cord or yarn, a crochet hook, scissors, and any additional embellishments you may want to add, such as beads or charms. Macramé cord is typically made of cotton or nylon and comes in various thicknesses and colors, allowing you to customize your projects to your liking.

Once you have your supplies ready, you can begin by learning the basic macramé crochet knots. The most common knots used in macramé crochet are the square knot, half knot, and double half hitch knot. These knots form the foundation of many macramé designs and can be combined in different ways to create various patterns and textures.

For a simple keychain project, you can start by creating a basic square knot pattern. Begin by cutting two equal lengths of macramé cord, approximately 12 inches each. Fold the cords in half and attach them to a keyring or lobster clasp using a lark's head knot. Then, start creating square knots by crossing the left cord over the middle cords and under the right cord, and then crossing the right cord over the middle cords and through the loop created by the left cord. Repeat this process until you reach your desired length, and finish off the keychain by tying a knot and trimming any excess cord.

Bracelets can be made using similar techniques, but with longer lengths of cord and additional knots or patterns. You can experiment with different knot combinations, such as alternating square knots, spiral knots, or even adding beads or charms for extra flair. The possibilities are endless, and you can let your creativity run wild.

As you practice and gain more experience, you can challenge yourself by trying more complex macramé crochet projects, such as plant hangers, wall hangings, or even clothing accessories.

Techniques for Adding Intricacy and Detail of Macramé Knotting: Macramé knotting is a versatile and creative craft that allows individuals to create intricate and detailed designs using various knotting techniques. Whether you are a beginner or an experienced macramé artist, there are several techniques that can be employed to add complexity and detail to your macramé projects.

One technique that can be used to add intricacy to macramé knotting is the use of different types of knots. There are numerous types of knots that can be incorporated into macramé designs, such as the square knot, the half knot, the double half hitch, and the lark's head knot, among others. By combining these knots in different ways, you can create unique patterns and textures in your macramé work.

Another technique that can be employed to add detail to macramé knotting is the use of different materials. While traditional macramé is often done using natural fibers such as cotton or hemp, incorporating different materials such as beads, feathers, or even metal accents can elevate the level of intricacy in your designs. These additional materials can be incorporated into the knots themselves or used as embellishments to add detail and visual interest to your macramé projects.

Additionally, varying the thickness and color of the cords used in macramé knotting can also contribute to the overall intricacy and detail of the design. By using cords of different thicknesses, you can create contrast and dimension in your macramé work. Similarly, incorporating cords of different colors can add visual interest and complexity to your designs.

Furthermore, experimenting with different patterns and designs can also enhance the intricacy and detail of macramé knotting. There are countless patterns and designs available for macramé, ranging from simple geometric shapes to more intricate and complex motifs. By exploring different patterns and designs, you can push the boundaries of your macramé skills and create stunning pieces that showcase your creativity and attention to detail.

Lastly, practicing patience and precision is crucial when aiming to add intricacy and detail to macramé knotting. Macramé is a craft that requires careful attention to detail and precise knotting techniques. Taking the time to ensure that each knot is executed correctly and that the tension is consistent throughout the piece will result in a more intricate and detailed final product.

In conclusion, there are several techniques that can be employed to add intricacy and detail to macramé knotting.

Combining Macramé and Crochet: Combining Macramé and Crochet is a creative and unique way to enhance your crafting skills and create stunning pieces of art. Macramé and crochet are both textile techniques that involve using knots and loops to create intricate patterns and designs. By combining these two techniques, you can add depth, texture, and visual interest to your projects.

Macramé is a technique that uses various knots to create decorative patterns and designs. It involves using cords or ropes and tying them together in specific ways to form knots and create intricate patterns. Macramé can be used to make anything from wall hangings and plant hangers to jewelry and accessories. It is a versatile technique that allows for endless creativity and customization.

On the other hand, crochet is a technique that uses a hook and yarn to create fabric. It involves pulling loops of yarn through other loops to create stitches. Crochet can be used to make a wide range of items, including blankets, scarves, hats, and clothing. It is a popular technique that is known for its versatility and ability to create intricate and detailed designs.

When combining macramé and crochet, you can incorporate macramé knots and techniques into your crochet projects or vice versa. For example, you can add macramé knots as decorative elements to a crochet wall hanging or use crochet stitches to create a base for a macramé plant hanger. The possibilities are endless, and you can experiment with different combinations to create unique and personalized pieces.

One way to combine macramé and crochet is by using macramé knots to create decorative borders or accents on crochet projects. For instance, you can add a macramé fringe to the edge of a crochet blanket or use macramé knots to create a decorative trim on a crochet scarf. This combination adds texture and visual interest to your crochet projects, making them stand out and look more intricate.

Another way to combine macramé and crochet is by using crochet stitches to create a base for macramé projects. For example, you can crochet a circular or rectangular base and then use macramé knots to create a hanging planter or a decorative wall hanging. This combination allows you to incorporate the stability and structure of crochet with the decorative and intricate patterns of macramé.

Combining macramé and crochet also opens up opportunities for incorporating different materials into your projects. While crochet traditionally uses yarn, macramé often involves working with cords or ropes.

CHAPTER ONE
Introduction

In this ultimate step-by-step macramé guide, you'll learn how to tie the basic macramé knots for beginners.

When you first begin learning macramé, it might be overwhelming to attempt to master all of the different macramé knots.

The lark's head knot, cow hitch knot, square knot, double half hitch knot, and wrapping knot are the five most important macramé knots for novices to learn.

You can find the five fundamental macramé knots in the next chapter with pictorial project guide!

After mastering the fundamental knots, you'll want to learn several intermediate knots such as the berry knot, vertical double half hitch, and diagonal double half hitch.

This macramé knot tutorial guide will demonstrate how to tie 15 common macramé knots in the various DIY projects in this book.

CHAPTER TWO

Basic macramé knots and patterns projects

Macrame Knots

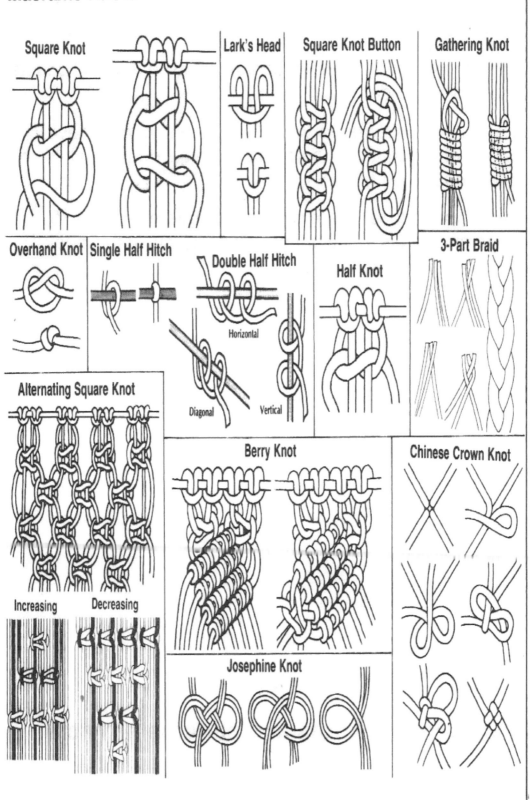

Square Knot

Lark's Head

Square Knot Button

Gathering Knot

Overhand Knot

Single Half Hitch

Double Half Hitch

Horizontal

Diagonal

Vertical

Half Knot

3-Part Braid

Alternating Square Knot

Increasing

Decreasing

Berry Knot

Chinese Crown Knot

Josephine Knot

I've included images for each macramé in this project, as well as a step-by-step written instruction with photos for this list of popular knots to get you started!

Knot of the Lark's Head

Fold your rope in half to create a Lark's Head Knot. Then wrap the loop around the dowel and behind it. Pull the rope's ends through the loop and tighten.

This common knot is used to secure cords to dowel rods or metal hoops for macrame wall hangings.

Knot of the Lark's Head in the vertical position (Vertical Lark's Head Knot)

1.

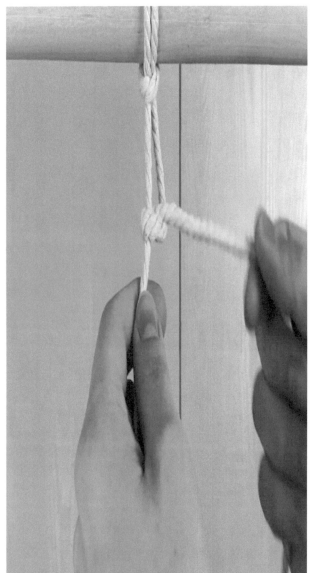

2.

•

3.

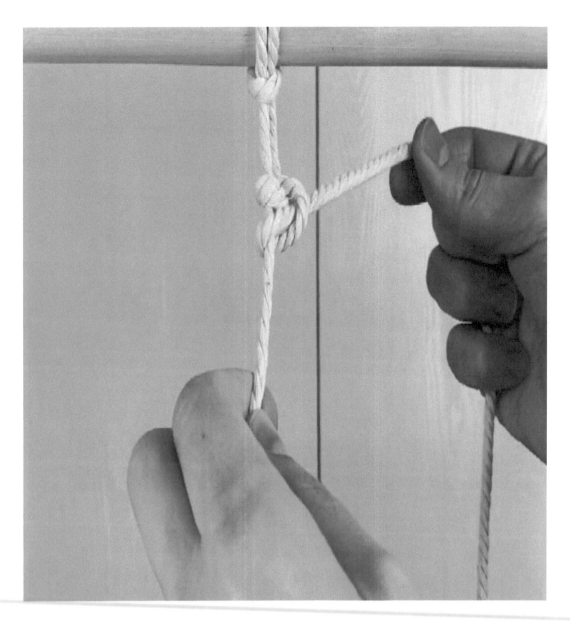

4.

To tie a Vertical Larks Head Knot on the right, bend the right cord in front of the left chord in a "L" form. Then loop the right cord's end behind and through the loop.

Reposition the right cord in the shape of a "L" behind the left cord. Tighten the end by wrapping it around in front of the cord and through the opening.

Hitch Knot in a Cow

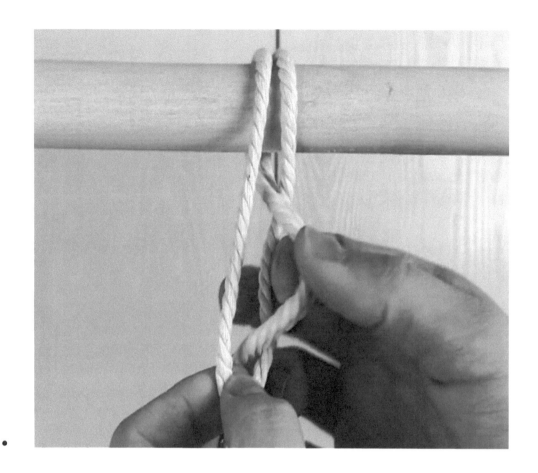

The Cow Hitch Knot is similar to the Larks Head knot, except that the folded end is brought up behind and over the dowel, facing the opposite direction.

Rectangular Knot or square knots

1.

2.

3.

4.

5.

6. Four cords will be required to tie a Square Knot. Your working cords will be on the left and right, and your filler cords will be in the center.

Bend the left cord forward and beneath the right cord, in front of the two center filler cords.

Then, with the right cord, bring it behind the filler cords and up through the loop created with the left cord. Tighten. A half knot is what this is.

To finish the square knot, create another half knot, but this time in the reverse direction.

Bring the right cord forward and under the left cord, in front of the filler cords.

At this point, easily bring the left chord behind the center cords and through the left cord's loop, and then tighten.

Depending on your location, this classic macramé knot can be used to create simple designs or intricate patterns.

Square Knot, Alternating

Alternating Square Knots are created by alternately using different cords in each row.

Square knots will be used as normal for the first row.

After that, skip the first two cords and begin your square knots for the second row.

On the third row, you'll return to the first pattern, and on the fourth row, you'll repeat the second-row pattern. This method results in an attractive mesh design.

Double Half Hitch

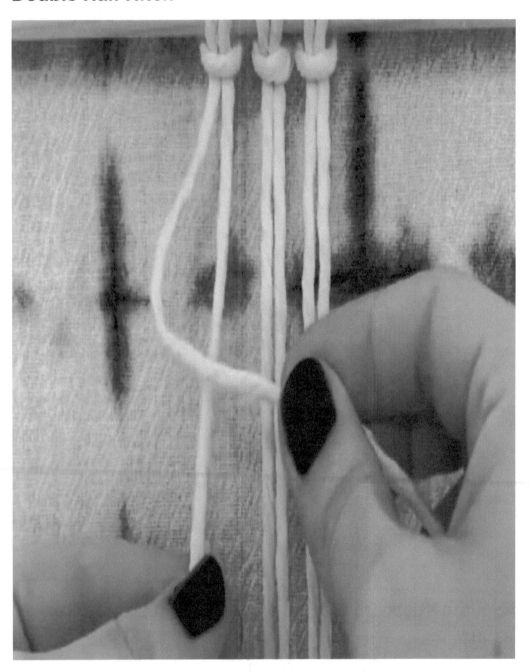

1.

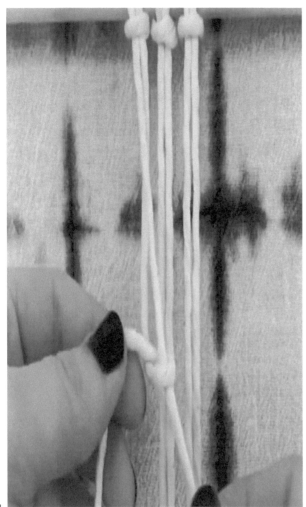

2.

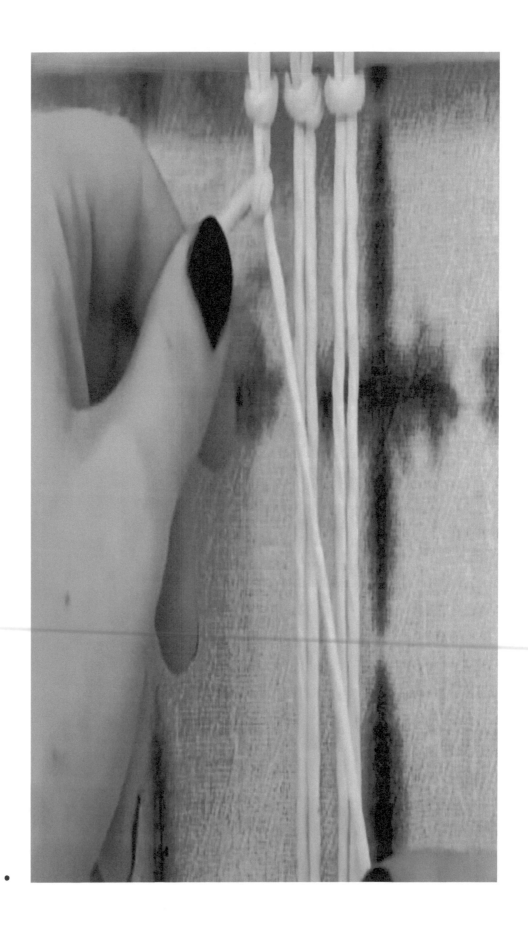

3.

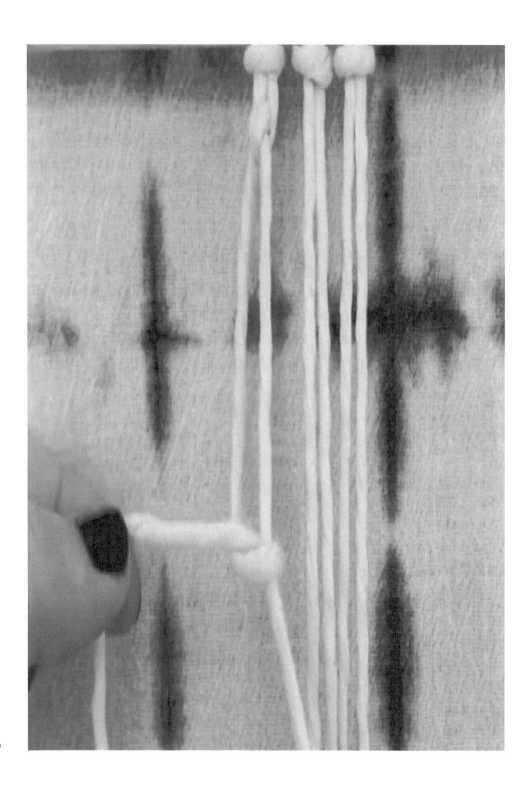

•

4.

To make a Double Half Hitch Knot (aka Clove Hitch Knot), you'll have a filler cord and a working cord. In the example above, I'm knotting to my right hand side. The technique is the same while heading to the left, but reversed.

First, hold the filler cord out straight (in this case, the right cord) (in this case, the right cord.)

Take the left cord and cross it across the right cord. Draw the end of the left cord over and through the loop created and pull it tight. You can easily slide the loop to wherever direction you desire the knot to be.

Repeat that technique again the same way and tighten the loop.

You have now created a single double half hitch knot. To build the next one, you'll use the same filler cord as the previous one, but the working cord will be the next cord over. Each working cord should only have one double half hitch knot.

Double Hitch Diagonal

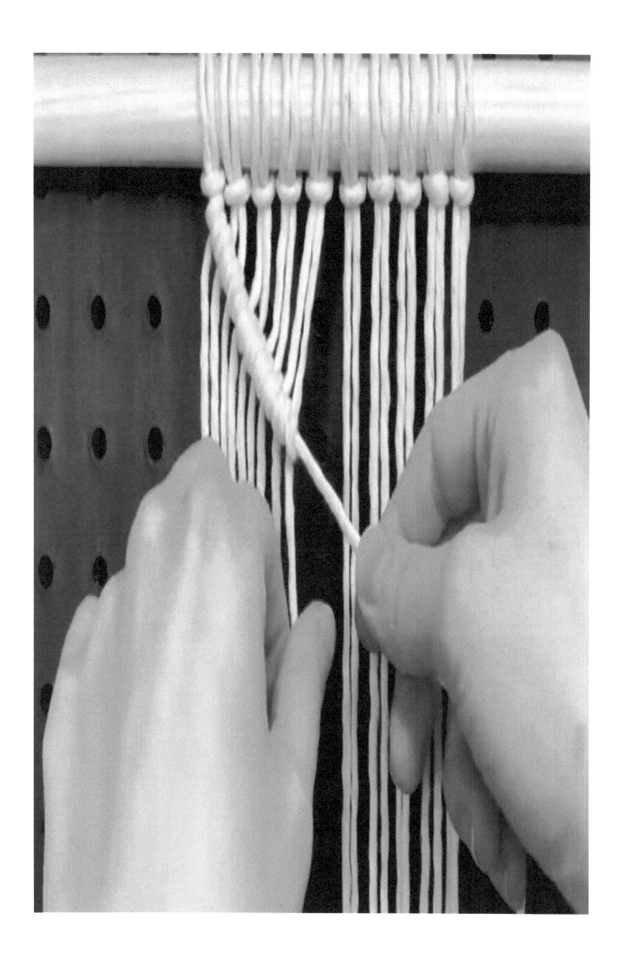

The Diagonal Half Hitch Knot is similar to the ordinary half hitch knot except that the filler rope is held at the angle desired for your row of knots.

• 1. Vertical Double Half Hitch

•

1.

•

2.

3.

•

4.

5.

•

6.

7.

8.

.

9.

•

10.

•

11.

•

12.

•

13.

14.

15.

16.

Although the Vertical Half Hitch Knot appears to be complex, it is actually rather simple. This knot is an excellent way to include color into your macramé creations.

To begin, you'll need a separate piece of rope to use as your working cord I'm using the orange cord in the picture above.

To begin, secure the working cord underneath the initial pair of filler cords. Thread the long end through the loop in front of and around the first set of filler cords. Tighten the knot and move it to the end position.

Continue to repeat this procedure until the first double half hitch knot is formed.

Bring the working cord behind the next filler cords, wrap it around the front of the filler cords while gripping the working chord's right side to form a loop, and draw the end through the loop.

Then, reposition the working cord in front of the filler cords, wrap it around, and draw it through the loop.

Continue with the next set of filler cords and repeat until the row is complete.

At the final pair of filler cords, tie the first half of the double half hitch knot as before, but then draw the working cable's end to the left side behind the filler cord.

Then, from left to right, bring the working cord in front of the filler cords and pull it through the loop.

Continue the next row to the left, passing below and around the filler cords for the first half of the knot then in front of and around for the second.

While this may look complex when written out, it's simpler than it appears. With this technique, you may create a stunning design!

Spiral with a Half Knot

Spiral left

•Right-spiraling spiral

A Half Knot Spiral is constructed by inverting the first half of a square knot and continuing the process for each succeeding knot and all subsequent knots.

The spiral's direction will be determined by whether you begin with your half knot on the right or left.

Spiral with a Half Hitch

The Half Hitch Spiral Knot is identical to the Half Knot Spiral, except that it is constructed entirely of half hitches.

Simply repeat tying a half hitch on the same filler cord and it will automatically spiral.

Berry Knot

•

•

To begin, tie three or four square knots. In this case, I began with three.

Thread the two center cords up and through the middle of the first square knot.

Pull down to roll the berry knot up and then secure it with a half knot beneath the berry knot.

• • **Barrel Knot**

•

To tie a Barrel Knot, begin by creating a loop with your cord and crossing the end in front, as seen in the first illustration.

Then, wrap the rope's end three times around and through the loop. It will resemble the second image.

Retain both ends and pull until it resembles the third image.

The wrapping Knot

•

1.

●

2.

3.

•

4.

5.

•

6.

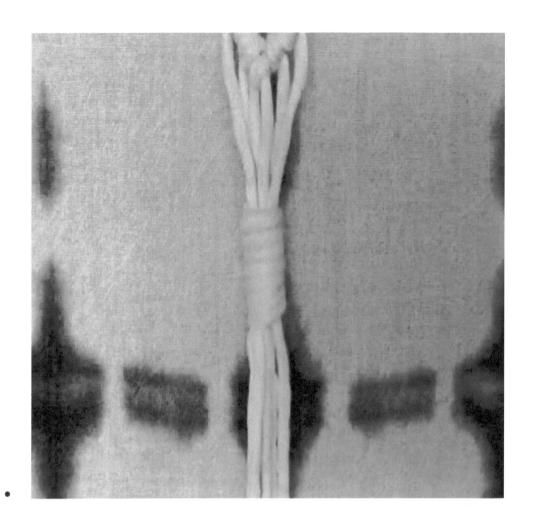

7.

To tie a Wrapping Knot, you'll need an extra foot or so of cord depending on the number of wraps you're planting and the thickness of the cord.

With one end of the cord, form it into a "U" shape. With the short and long ends of the "U" shaped chord facing up, and the bent "U" section facing down, place it against the filler cords (all the cords you'll be wrapping around).

With the long end of the wrapping cable, begin winding around all of the cords (including the short end). Each wrap should be snug against the preceding one, but not overlapping.

Once you've completed seven to ten wraps (or as many as you like), thread the wrapping cord through the loop created by the bottom of the "U."

To tighten the loop, pull on the top cord that protrudes from the wraps (the short end of the working cord).

Continue dragging the top cord upward until the loop is about halfway into the wraps. You do not want it to protrude above the wraps' top.

Trim the cord's two ends and insert them into the wraps.

• • Overhand Knot

•

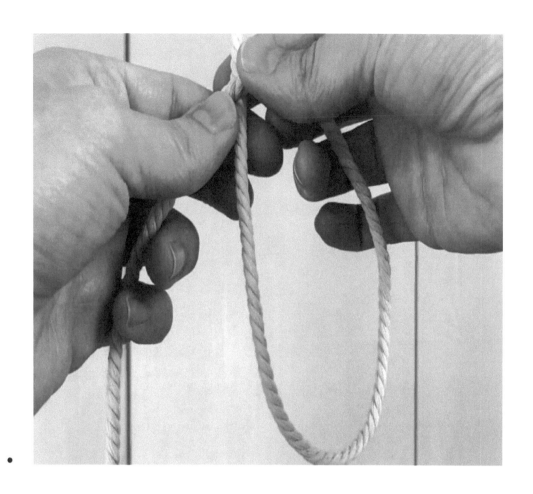

The Overhand Knot is a really simple knot that you are probably already familiar with.

Simply create a loop and pull the ends through. The first one is created with two cords, while the second one is made with a single cord. Simple peasy.

• 1. Constrictor Knot

1.

2.

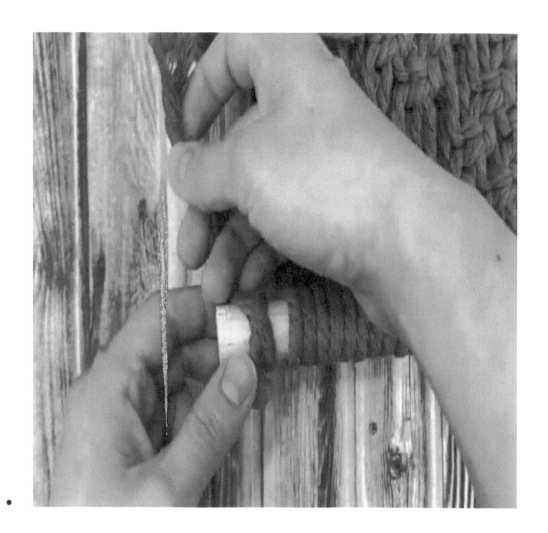

•

3.

4.

5.

6.

-

7.

The Constrictor Knot is an excellent knot to use when attaching a hanging rope to your completed macrame product.

In the images above, I'm working on the reverse side of my macrame piece.

You'll need a length of string to serve as a hanger, the length of which will depend on the length of your creation. The knots will not consume an excessive amount of string.

As seen in the first photo, begin on the left side by holding the cord in front of the dowel with the short end facing up.

Wrap it around the dowel, as shown in the second photo.

Wrap it around the dowel once more, crossing the initial wrap over to form a "X" and bringing the end to the left.

Bring the short end of the cable in front of the long end, and then push the short end under and through the "X."

Tighten both ends of the cord and repeat with the other end of the cord on the opposite side of the dowel.

Once the hanger is attached, I trim the short ends to about an inch or two and glue them to the back of the dowel to prevent them from hanging down.

CHAPTER THREE

How to Make a Jute Macramé Tote Bag

I've always been a fan of string shopping bags. What better way to demonstrate how healthy you are than to display your fruit and vegetable haul? Simply conceal the unhealthy food in a cloth tote! But truly, anything that reminds me to bring my reusable shopping bags to the grocery is a plus.

I crocheted one for myself in the traditional method a few years ago and still use it frequently. As this was such a success, I decided to repeat it. This time, we're adding a twist to the bag by employing a macrame knotting technique. To expedite the procedure, I utilized a thick jute rope and these Hobbycraft bag handles, which allowed me to whip up this bag in under an hour and be out the door.

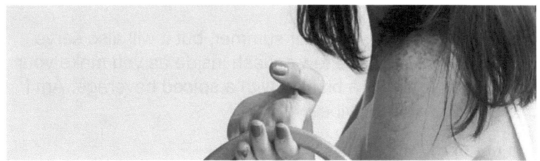

This purse looks fantastic suited for summer, but it will also serve you well in the fall. Consider a few squash inside as you make your way home to curl up under a blanket with a spiced beverage. Am I starting to give you autumn vibes yet?

Materials needed

Jute Rope Handles for the Bag

Procedures:

Step 1: Cut ten 2.3-metre-long strands of rope. They can be folded in half and threaded through the gap on the bag handle with the folded center. Pass the rope's ends through the loop created in the preceding step. Strike hard. This procedure should be repeated until each bag handle has five pieces of rope attached.

Step 2: Beginning at one end, cut two lengths of rope and push the remainder to one side. With these two parts, we're going to tie our first knot. This is the knot we'll use throughout the instruction, so if you get stuck, refer to the following few stages.

Make a right angle crossing with the right strand over the left rope.

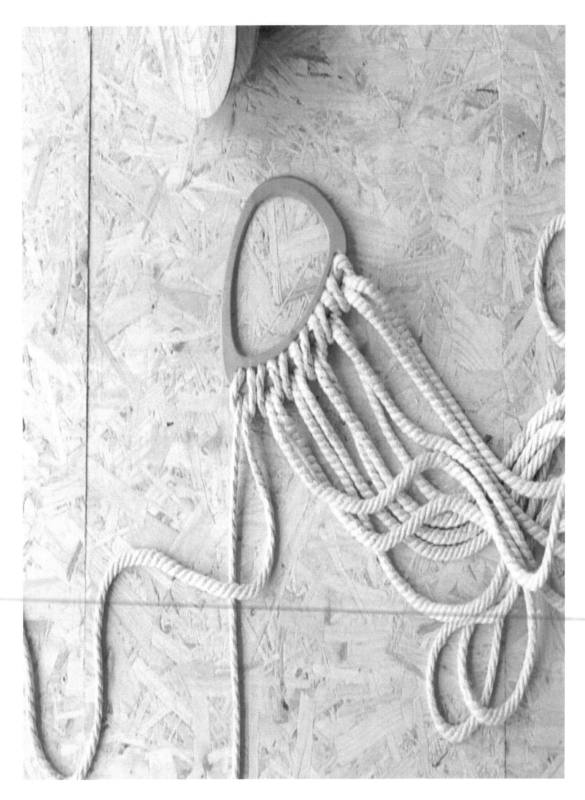

Thread the left rope through the space created by the two ropes. Pull the rope's ends apart until the knot forms and is in the proper location. It should be approximately five centimeters from the handle.

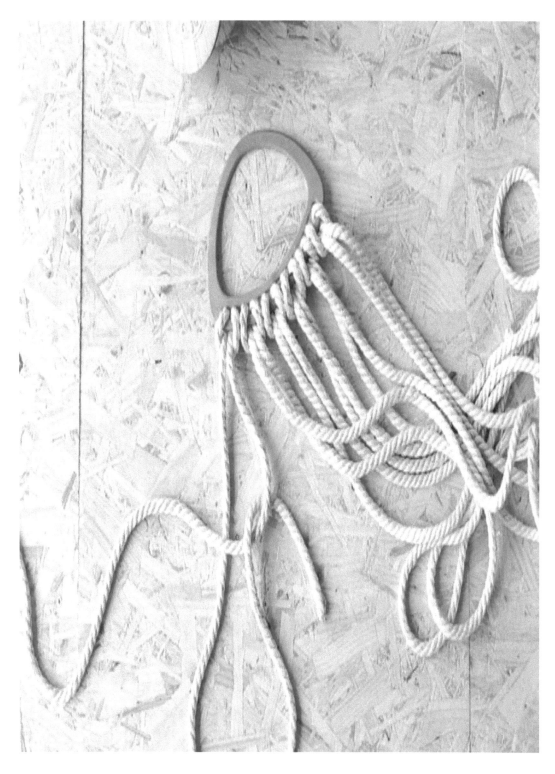

To finish the knot, cross the left hand rope over the right.

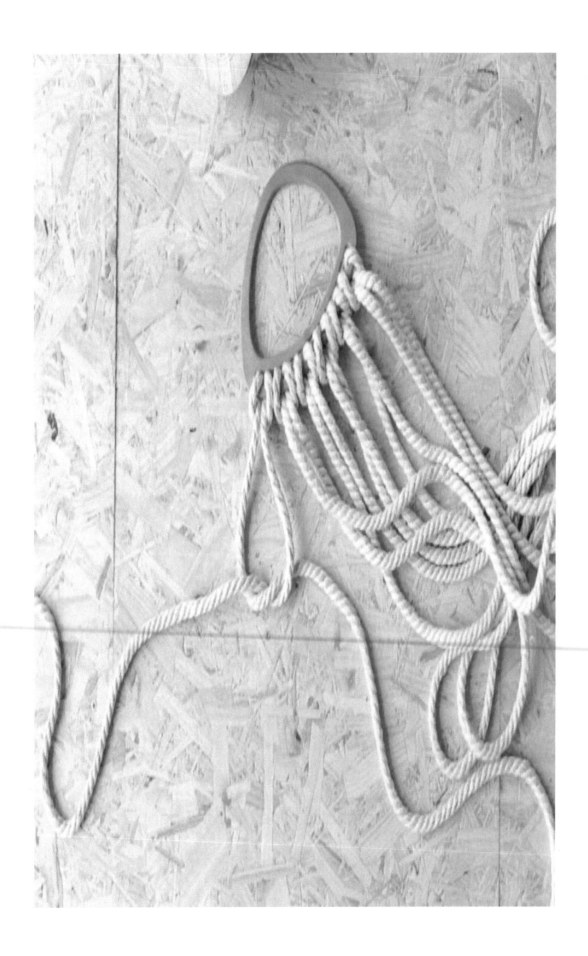

This time, thread the rope on the right through the gap. Again, tighten the knot. This is now a double half hitch knot that has been completed.

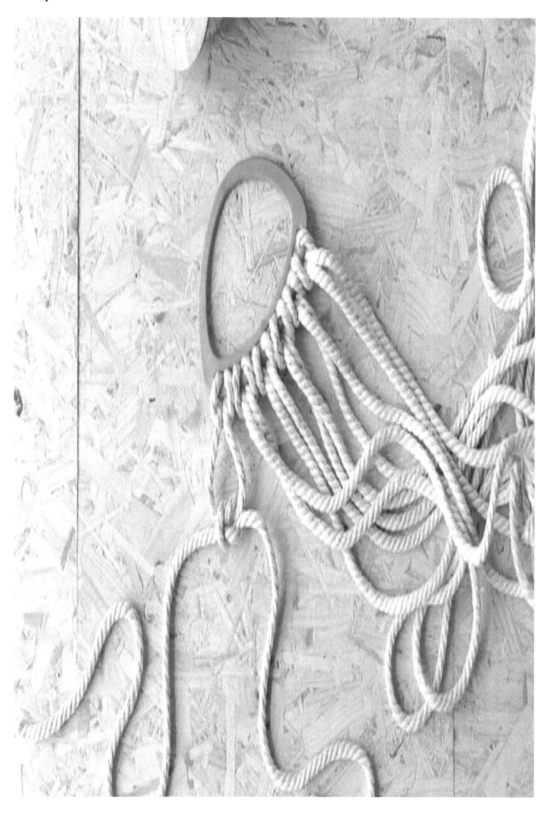

Step 3: Using the remaining ropes on the handle, create four more of these knots in a row. Then repeat the procedure, omitting the first rope and knotting the second and third. Along the row, continue. This time, tie four knots and leave the first and final ropes untied.

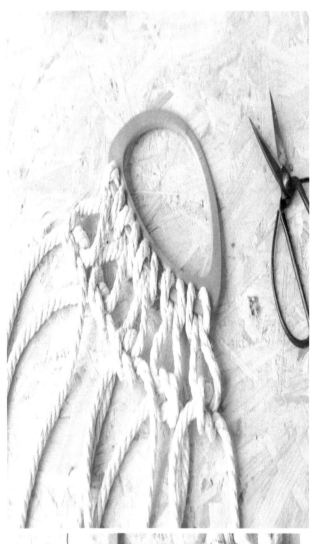

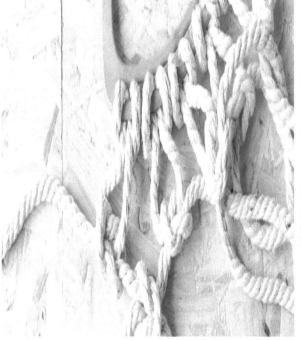

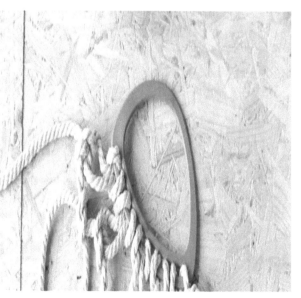

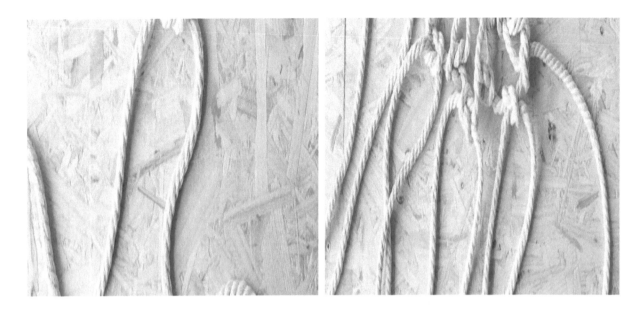

Step 4: Once the second row is complete, repeat the process for the third row so five knots, without missing any ropes.

Step 5: When the third row is complete, proceed to the second handle and repeat steps 2-4. Once that is complete, align the two handles so that their back sides face each other.

Step 6: To begin the following row, knot together the bag's two end ropes from the front and back. Reverse the knots along the front and

back of the ropes until you reach the opposite end. The final ropes on the front and back should then be removed. Bundle these.

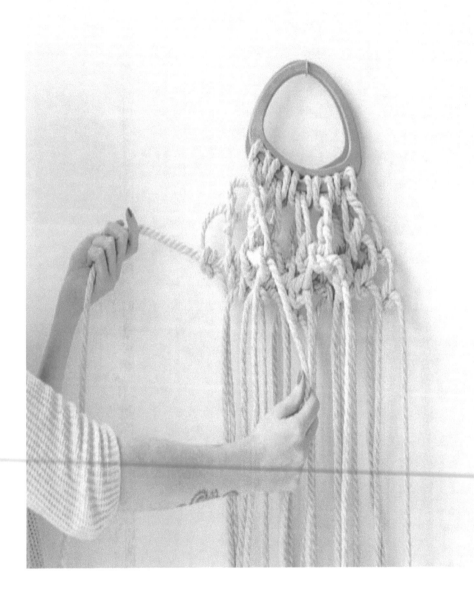

Step 7: Continue knotting in this pattern until the strands have approximately 10cm of rope remaining.

Step 8: Cut a four-metre-long piece of rope. Utilize the same technique as for the handles to attach this to the final side knot.

Step 9: Wrap the rope around a front strand and a back strand. Tie one double half hitch knot, then repeat with two additional knots (one in front and one in back). Maintain your efforts until the task is completed.

Step10: Untangle the rope that is dangling. To keep them in place, tie strands of these together with knots. To reinforce these, you can add some glue. Create a fringe by combing it out.

And that concludes the construction of your bag. If you're looking for something with a pop of color, try dying it with a natural burnt red or sage green dye.

CHAPTER FOUR

How to macramé Lace Planter

Lace Planter hanger has a sensitive look; it functions short sennits of square knots in addition to areas without knots.

This plant hanger design appears better with plant pots or bowls which can be as a minimum 10 inches extensive. The cradle component at the bottom can be adjusted for any pinnacle.

This Macrame sample is straightforward to make, but high-quality tuning the location of the knots takes greater time.

The finished period is approximately 50 inches, which incorporates the perimeter at the lowest.

To prolong this plant hanger, you may tie extra knots in the sennits, or boom the spacing between them.

make certain you narrow the cords longer in case you make modifications to the size.

Required Materials

- 4mm Macramé twine (seventy five yards)

- One 2-inch Ring

- One 2.5-inch Ring

- Measuring tape

- project Board and Pins

- 24 small beads for fringe (elective)

- Protective Tape and Rubber Bands

Knots Used:

- Double half of Hitch (DHH)

- Rectangular Knot (SK)

- Wrapped Knot

- Alternating square Knots

- Overhand Knot

- Barrel Knot

Mounting Procedures

Step 1: reduce 12 cords, every 6 yards long. put together the pointers with covering tape to save you unraveling. As you apply the tape, compress the cease to make it as slim as feasible (for beading).

lessen 2 cords, every 36 inches long (for Wrapped Knots).

Step 2: Fold the 6-yard cords in half of of and function them over the bottom of the two-inch ring, at the equal time as keeping the hoop upright.

Very important: once you installation each twine onto the ring, fit the ends to middle it. Then roll up the wire and cozy it with a rubber band. try this with every cord.

Cautiously location the set up cords on your project board, as demonstrated inside the photo below; The Wrapped Knot at the pinnacle of the Lace Planter is less hard to make on a surface, so you can use pins.

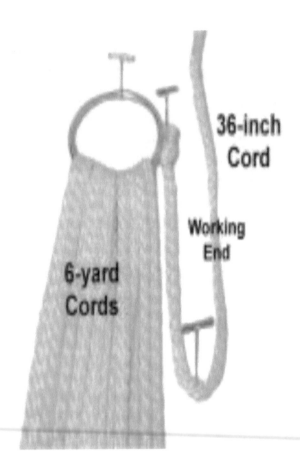

36-inch
Cord

Working
End

6-yard
Cords

Make sure secure a 36-inch wire to the proper of the hoop. bring it down three inches, then fold it and flow into it again up. comfy it at the fold.

This cord is used to make the Wrapped knot, defined below.

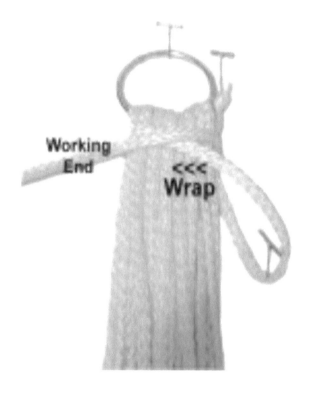

pass the 36-inch twine (running cease) to the left, over the the front of all of the cords.

Carry it underneath all of the cords, then back to the the the front.

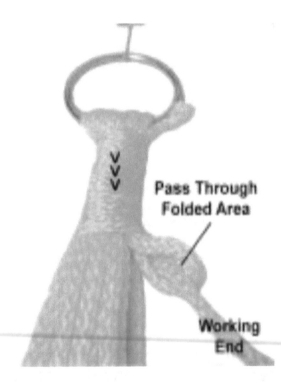

Pass Through
Folded Area

Working
End

Now wrap several more times, moving downward, till the knot is at least one point five (1.5) inches lengthy.

Skip the operating surrender via the folded place, which looks as if a loop.

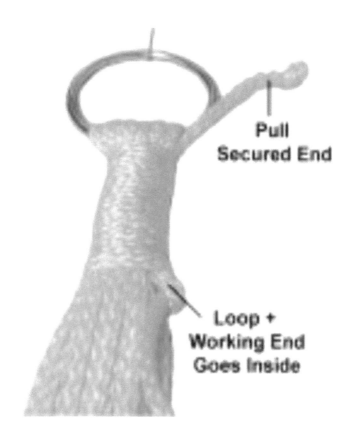

Pull
Secured End

Loop +
Working End
Goes Inside

Eliminate the pin from the secured cease of the 36-inch wire. Pull it gradually, so the loop and running quit circulate into the Wrapped Knot. stop pulling while the loop is ready 1/2 manner through the knot.

Cut off the 2 ends flush with the pinnacle and bottom of the knot. Use tweezers to push the stubs in the wrapped detail.

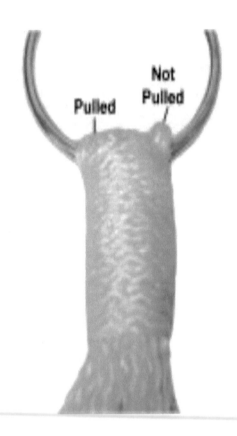

Step three: Unroll each of the lengthy cords and pull both HALVES at the same time, so the wire tightens throughout the hoop above the Wrapped Knot.

This photograph suggests most of the cords already accomplished, but I left one so that you may want to see how free it'd be if you did now not pull the cords.

Pinnacle place

Hold up the cords through the ring on the pinnacle.   The the rest of the Lace Planter is much less hard to finish with the cords dangling.

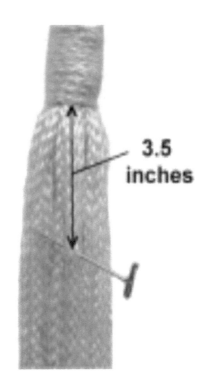

3.5
inches

Step 4: pick one of the long cords and diploma from the Wrapped
Knot down three.5 inches.

area a pin (or tape) horizontally, to mark that spot.

Skip all the cords into the two point five-inch ring, while preserving it
degree with the ground (see subsequent photo and discover the
marked cord, and connect it to the ring with a Double half Hitch.

The pins need to be as near the hoop as viable earlier than you
tighten the 2 half Hitches see photograph below.

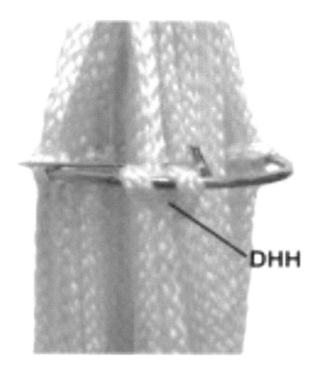

DHH

Step five: Repeat step four with all the other cords, attaching them to the equal ring one after the other.

Measuring every twine is important to make certain the Lace Planter is stage, so make the effort and be accurate.

And when you are finished, you can add extra half of Hitches if the ring is not absolutely blanketed.

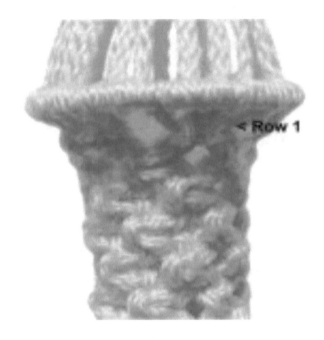

< Row 1

Step 6: Tie 6 rows of Alternating rectangular Knots, placing the first row as close to the ring as possible. each knot should have 2 walking cords and a pair of fillers.

make sure you tighten every knot firmly so they may be close together. this will cause the top portion of the Lace Planter to curve inward slightly.

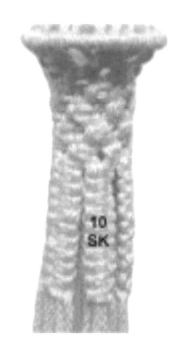

Step 7: Divide the cords into 6 organizations of 4 cords.

With each corporation, tie a sennit of 10 square Knots. Push them close together as you improvement, so there aren't any gaps.

critical: diploma every sennit to be sure they may be the same period. you can make changes via pushing the knots closer collectively or moving them apart slightly.

measure from the pinnacle of the primary knot to the lowest of the final.

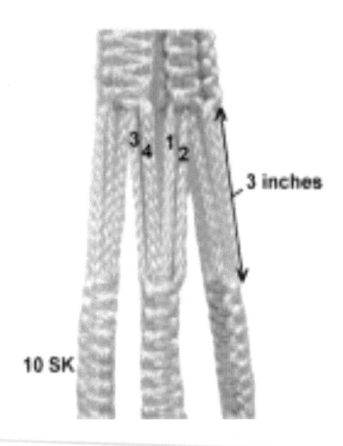

Step eight: pick out sennits that relaxation next to every other and mentally extensive variety the cords in every 1 - 4.

alternate by means of combining cords three - 4 from the sennit on your left, with 1 - 2 from the most effective at the right.

Step eight, continued: flow into down three inches, and tie any other sennit with 10 SK.

keep the fillers even as tightening each knot, so the anxiety in all four cords is the same Push the knots close together, however be cautious you do not exchange the position of the first knot.

Step 9: Repeat step eight with all of the different sennits. diploma to ensure they are all 3 inches under the sennits made in step 7.

important: measure every sennit and alter them as wished, so they are all of the identical duration.

that is one of the most crucial elements to correctly making the Lace Planter, so degree carefully.

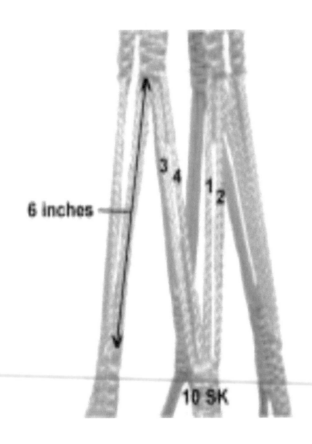

6 inches

Step 10: Repeat step 8, alternating the cords once more.

Move down 6 inches, then tie the SK sennit with 10 knots.

Repeat with the closing cords.

Step eleven: Create the following phase for the Lace Planter through repeating step 8 (alternating the cords).

Circulate down 9 inches, and tie 2 SK.

Repeat with all of the remaining cords.

Cradle

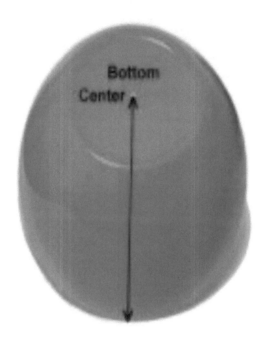

Bottom Center

Step 12: measure the bowl or pot you advise to apply on your Lace Planter. start at the top component, and bring the tape degree to the lowest center factor.

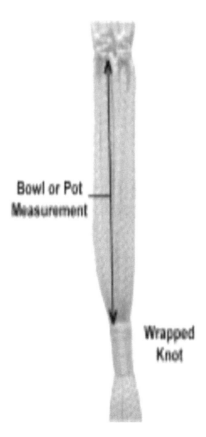

Bowl or Pot Measurement

Wrapped Knot

The cradle needs to be close to that measurement.

Step 13: The cradle for the Lace Planter is the region many of the two SK you tied in step eleven, and the Wrapped Knot you will now tie.

Set up all the cords so they'll be now not twisted. They should hang straight down from the SK. It facilitates if you installation 3 agencies inside the the the front and 3 in the back of them.

Pass down the identical distance because the pot size you obtain in step 12.

Tie a Wrapped Knot the use of the opposite 36-inch wire. It ought to be at least 1.5 inches lengthy. Ensure you wrap firmly, so it's miles tight.

Do not reduce off the ends after it's far tightened.

Step 14: area the pot or bowl in the cradle. the bottom ought to relaxation in competition to the Wrapped knot.

While the two SK you tied in step 11 need to be near the upper edge of the pot or bowl.

Also you could lightly slide the Wrapped Knot up or down as needed to gather the superb placement.

Crucial: Do not pull the cords, or the cradle becomes crooked as soon as you want the match, you may complete the Wrapped Knot thru lowering off the ends flush with the pinnacle and backside of the knot. Tuck the stubs in the wrapped region.

I propose you whole the Lace Planter thru creating a beaded fringe as defined below.

Its miles vital that you do no longer pull the cords, or the cradle turns into deformed while because of this, a brushed fringe is not endorsed.

Irrespective of what shape of fringe you are making, you want to complete off the cords in a few manner to prevent unraveling and you could practice completing knots, or paint the hints with glue or nail polish.

Even as the use of Bonnie Braid or similar synthetic fabric, you can melt the hints with a flame while taking a look at the cloth first to make sure it does no longer burn as usual.

Beaded Fringe knot tying

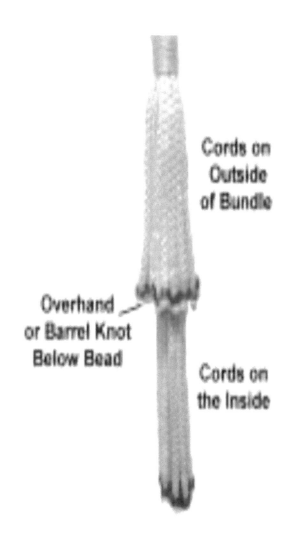

Cords on
Outside
of Bundle

Overhand
or Barrel Knot
Below Bead

Cords on
the Inside

Step 15: test the package deal of cords coming from the Wrapped Knot.

Some are at the out of doors of the group and others at the indoors.

Mark the cords on the outdoor with tape, because of the fact they may be used for the short fringe, that you create first.

Step 15, continued: diploma one marked wire from the Wrapped knot down at least four inches.

Slide a bead onto the twine, and tie either an Overhand or Barrel Knot beneath it. Be very careful while tightening, so you don't pull the twine downward too much.

Repeat the equal technique with the final marked cords and through measuring every one, the beads must all be on the same degree. Make changes if needed.

Step 16: Now you are making the lengthy fringe with the very last cords at the interior of the package deal to the degree one cord from the Wrapped Knot down at the least 8 inches while comply with the bead, followed by means of using the knot. Repeat with the alternative cords.

Step 17: as soon as all of the beads are on and in which you want them, lessen off the extra fabric. For Bonnie Braid or Nylon, you can melt the stub with a flame; hope you followed the steps in this project just in case you are not very clear with the steps taken you can read through again for more clarity. Thanks for reading for lets go to the next project.

CHAPTER FIVE

Mini Macramé Christmas Ornaments

Mini Macrame
Christmas Ornaments

I adore crafting a few homemade Christmas decorations each year, and this year these small macramé Christmas ornaments turned out so cute.

I'm joining in with the Seasonal Simplicity Christmas Series again this week, hosted by The Happy Housie. This week we're presenting Christmas Ornament ideas.

I had wanted to make these macramé Christmas decorations last year, and ran out of time to perfect them, so they were on the very top of my list this year. This year I got the perfect affordable rope at the dollar store Dollarama for my Canadian friends, and love how these turned out. They were incredibly affordable to create, and relatively easy once you got the hang of it. I am one of those folks that can't knit or crochet, so if you are in the same boat there's hope for you too.

These two designs require only three easy knots, the lark's head, the square knot, and the double half hitch -I'm not counting the diagonal half hitch, since it's merely a variation. Macramé is actually fairly straightforward once you get the hang of it. I've taken step by step images to aid, but if you're still struggling, just watch a little video on-line of the knot you're stuck on. Once you get it, you're good. It is making use of some of the above knot repeated.

Materials For Christmas Macramé Ornaments

• Masking tape

• Scissors

• Macramé cord or rope

• Twigs

• Hairbrush or comb

Getting the Cords On To The Twig

To get started cut a short twig and use the lark's head knot to attach 6 cords to the top. I used rope, but before I attached it to the twig I un-wound it and changed it from 3 ply to single ply. Each cord should be roughly 2 feet length.

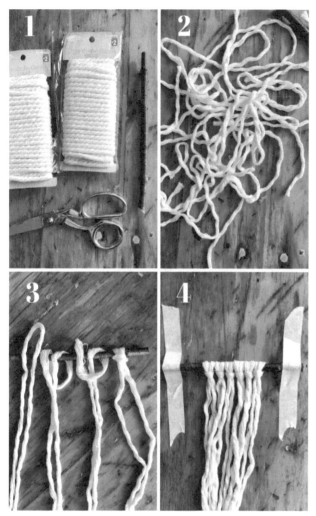

Fold the rope in half and lay the middle over the top of the twig to tie a lark's head knot.

Pull the two ends through the top and fold the loop over the back of the twig. Tighten the grip. Also repeat it with the remaining 6 cords.

Mini Macrame Square Knot Christmas Ornament

The very first square knot

Once the cords are secured to the twig, begin the first row, which will consist of three square knots. Start on the left and separate the first four cords, as these knots are tied with four cords.

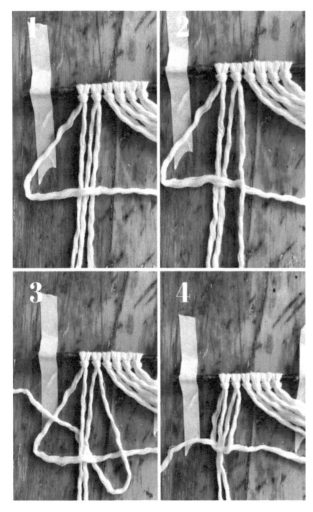

To make the square knot, grab the left hand cord and pull it out such that a number "4" shape forms.

Tuck the end of the first cord under the end of the fourth cord.

Then, bring the end of the fourth cord up and behind the middle two cords, as well as through the area between the first and second cords that resembles a four.

Pull the ends of the first and fourth cords together to tighten and move the knot to the top. This is the beginning of a square knot.

Do the same process for the second half of the square knot, but in the opposite direction. You'll make your "4" shape with the first and fourth cords, but with the "4" backwards and facing the right side.

Then cross the first cord over the fourth.

Then, feed the tail of the first cord through the aperture of the "4" form and under the second and third cords.

Tighten the ends of the first and fourth cords to form your first square knot.

Rows 1 through 3

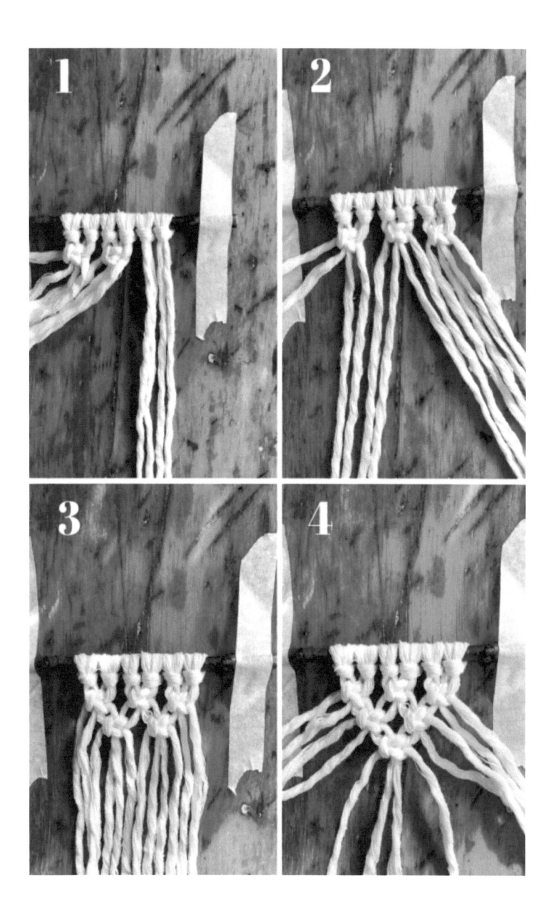

Continue working in four-cord portions. Tie another square knot and another square knot along the top row to form three.

The second row will consist of simply two square knots. Begin by separating out the first two cords. The following four cords are for the second square knot on row 2, followed by the following one. This will also leave the other two cables exposed on the other end.

To tie the third row, only use the row's center four cords.

You may need to alter your tension; try to maintain the knots evenly tightened and spaced.

4-5 rows

Row 4: Repeat row 2 with 2 square knots, omitting the two cords on either side.

Row 5 is a duplicate of row 1 with 3 square knots.

Half Hitch Knot Row 6

You could leave it at that with the square knots, or you could add a row of half hitch knots like I did.

To make a half hitch knot, grab the first string in the row and pull it horizontally across the item. This is your lead cord.

Take the second cord from behind, through the hole you've made, and over the lead. Repeat the knot with the same second cord. That's one-half of a hitch.

Continue along the rest of the cables, taking care to keep the lead cord level and straight while bending the remaining strands around it.

Pull the lead cord to tighten the knots.

Putting the Ornament Together

Finish by cutting the ends straight across or into a downward or upward "V" at the bottom.

Then, using a brushes or comb, remove the cord and make the fringe bottom.

After brushing it out, you may need to re-trim the shape somewhat.

Finally, trim the twig's ends and attach a length of cord to hang the ornament on.

The diagonal half hitch was used to make the second tiny macramé Christmas ornament I produced. It's similar to the half hitch we used on the first one, but on the diagonal.

Mini Macramé Ornament with a Diagonal Half Hitch

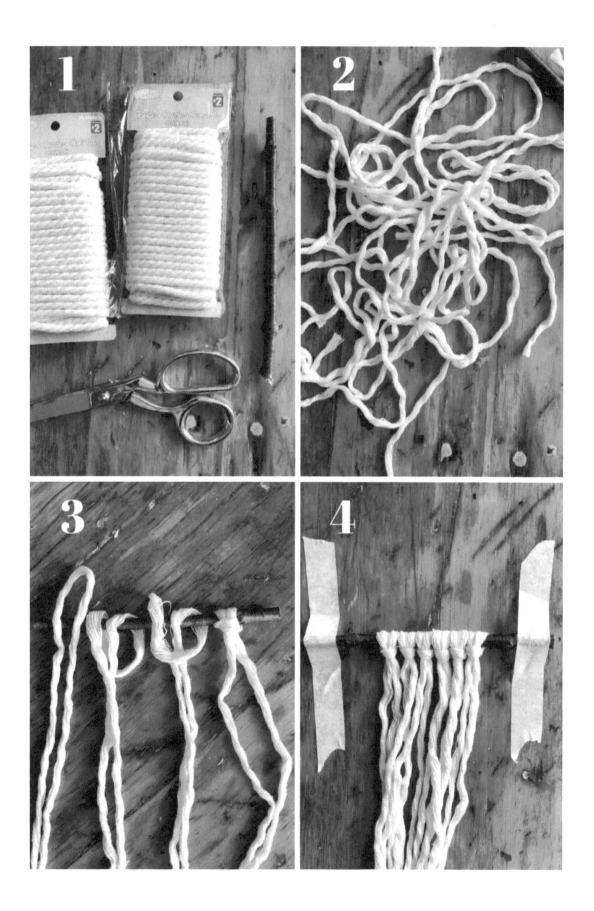

Begin by attaching 6 cords to a twig with a lark's knot, precisely like the first one.

Make three rows of diagonal half hitch knots to form a "V" for this decoration.

The first cord will be your lead cord; hold it diagonally this time rather than horizontally, and loop the second cord up and over it, through the hole you've made. Repeat with the second cord to complete the half hitch knot.

Tie a half hitch with the third cord somewhat further down, on the diagonal of your lead cord, while holding the lead rope securely at a diagonal.

Repeat same step for the first six cords.

Then take the last cord, the 12th cord on the far right, and use it as the lead cord, tying half hitches in the opposite way to meet in the center.

Rows 2 and 3

Ensure row 2 should be the same as row 1. But this time, when you meet in the center, you can use the cable from the opposite side to connect the two sides of the "V," as shown in picture 2 of the collage above.

To finish the ornament, trim the cord edges along the bottom and brush out the fringe like you did with the first one.

Finally, add a hanging string and cut the twig ends.

I really like how these small macrame Christmas tree ornaments turned out. On a cold night, they're the ideal little TV watching craft.

On a cold night, they're the ideal little TV watching craft. Because they are so little, they are also quite quick to create. They're so little and perfect for Barbie; my children were already eyeing them to use as wall hangings in their Barbie doll house.

I made three of each type, and they look fantastic on my Boho-themed Christmas tree. If you like the bohemian look for Christmas, you'll like my Black and White Boho Christmas Mantel.

Mini Macrame Christmas Ornaments are a simple DIY project.

175

If you're looking for additional ideas, be sure to check out all of these wonderful Christmas Ornament ideas.

CHAPTER SIX

Macramé wall hanging room divider project

Macramé wall hanging room divider format to weave onto the frame hanger; though what I clearly like most approximately about this format is that is, in spite of how complicated it looks even though it consists of one number one knot except for the Lark's Head Knot on the pinnacle and I need to strive this project however nevertheless intimidated allow me repeat that one of the primary Knot.

As lots as I love the half of Hitch Knot, I keep in mind it an intermediate skills. I desired to layout this folding screen for all and sundry, which include macramé novices, so I only used the rectangular Knot or a mild variant of it.

Required material for project tools

- 60 portions of 3/16″ cotton rope, measuring 25 ft. every

- overlaying tape for wrapping the ends of the ropes to prevent fraying in some unspecified time in the future of the weaving

- Scissors

- 2 yards of 60″ wide muslin cotton cloth

Step 1: – Lark's Head Knot

Tie 20 portions of 25′ cord to the primary panel, using the Lark's Head knot.

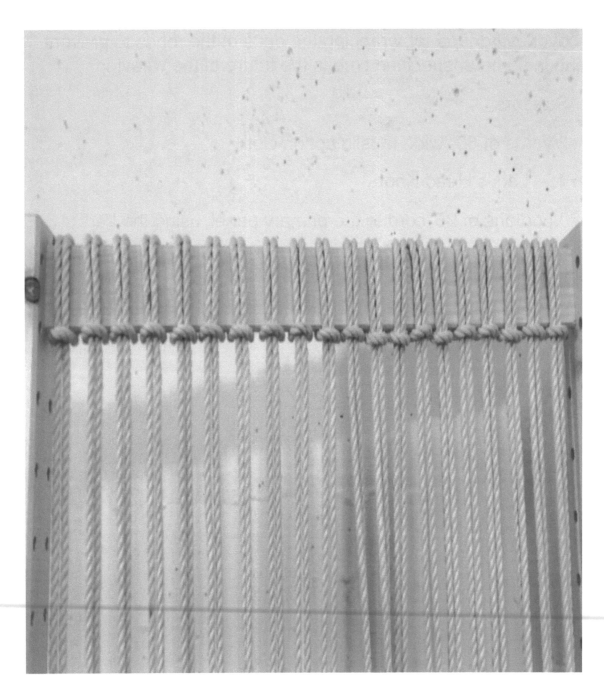

Step 2: – square Knot

starting with the primary individual wire on the left, make a horizontal row of 10 square Knots.

Step three: Developing a diamond format

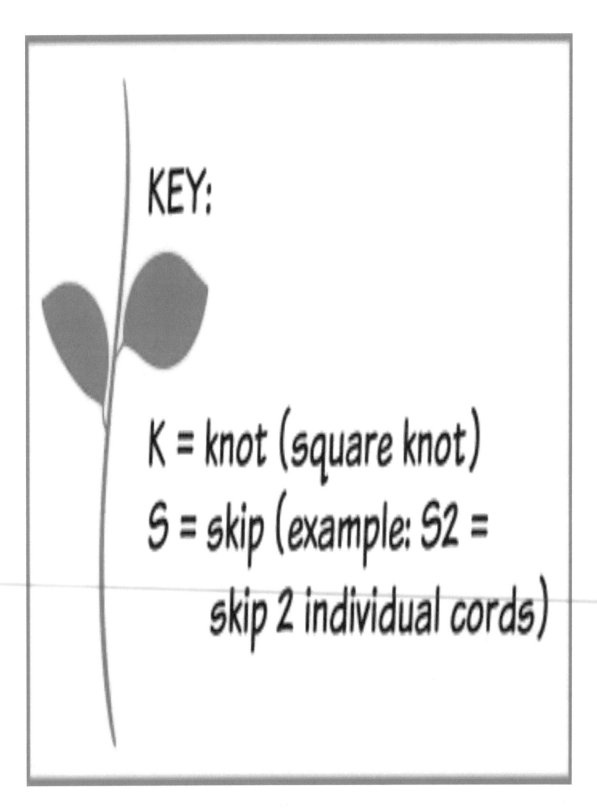

KEY:

K = knot (square knot)
S = skip (example: S2 = skip 2 individual cords)

Using of this key, comply with the commands below to make eleven horizontal rows. this can create a diamond sample.

- Row 1: Already finished beginning with 1st character cord on left, tie 10 square Knots

- Row 2: starting with third twine, tie nine Alternating square Knots

- Row 3: beginning with fifth cord, tie eight Alternating square Knots

- Row four: beginning with 7th cord, 3K – S4 – 3K – S6

- Row 5: beginning with 9th cord, 2K – S8 – 2K – S8

- Row 6: beginning with 11th wire, 1K – S12 – 1K – S10

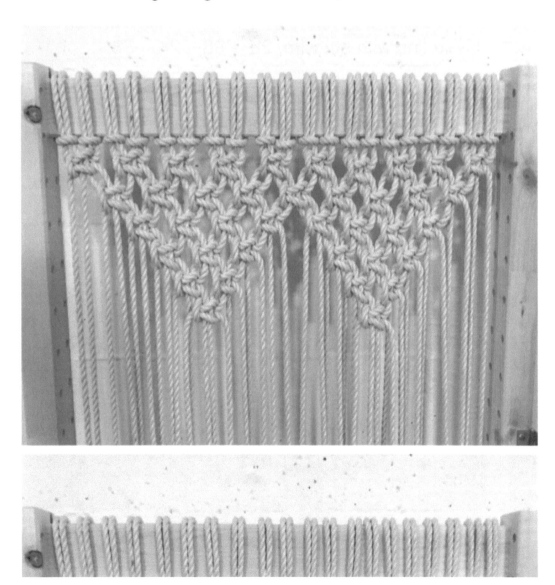

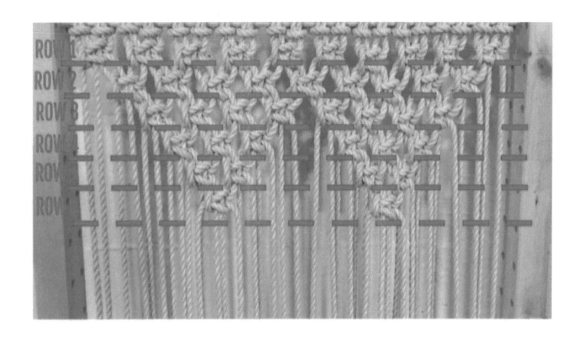

- Row 7:   beginning with 9th wire, 2K – S8 – 2K – S8

- Row 8:   starting with 7th wire, 3K – S4 – 3K – S6

- Row nine: starting with 5th twine, 8K – S4

- Row 10: beginning with 3rd wire, 9K – S2

- Row eleven: starting with 1st wire, 10K

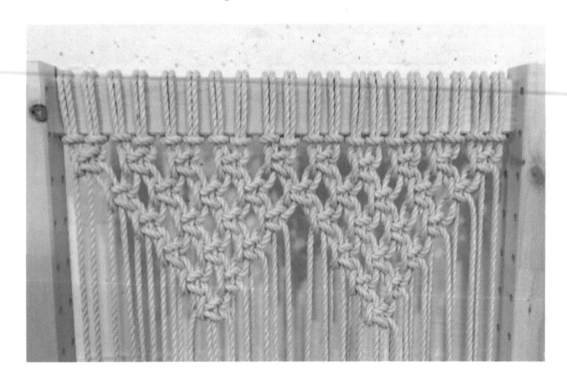

Step four: Add half square Spiral Knots

Don't be fooled thru the decision; you ought not to examine a brand new knot! The 1/2 square Spiral Knot is honestly a clean variant of the rectangular Knot. You've were given this!

Beneath your ultimate row of square Knots, beginning with the fifth person twine from the left, use the subsequent enterprise of 4 cords to tie a half of rectangular Spiral Knot. This is just like tying a vertical row of square Knots however continuously beginning from the identical side. Hold weaving this vertical row of spiral knots until you attain the top of the next crossbar at the wooden frame and pass the subsequent four person cords, then make each other vertical row of 1/2 of square Spiral Knots. Retain making greater vertical rows of spiral knots and skipping the required amount of cords as demonstrated within the photo beneath.

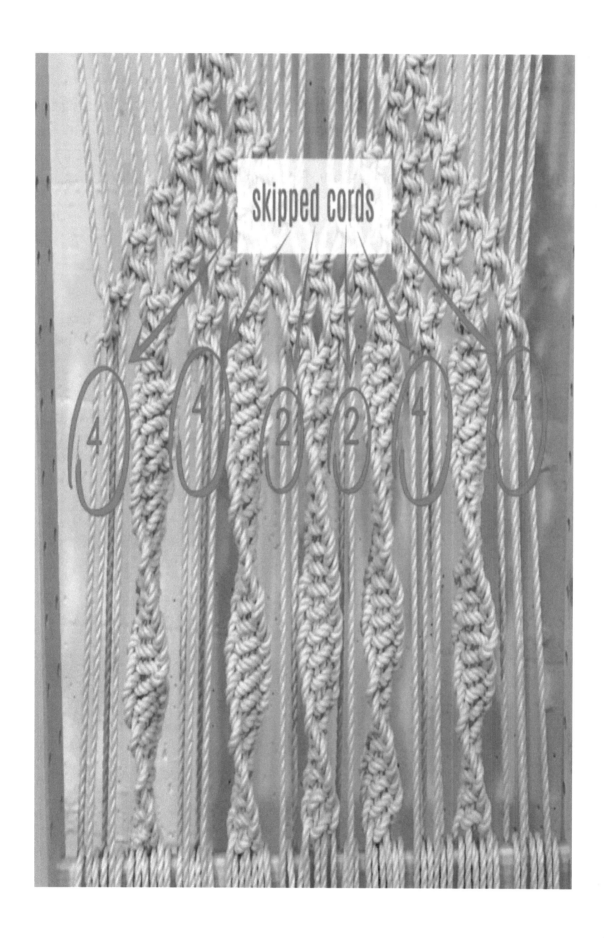

Step 5: completing pinnacle segment

to connect the pinnacle section of the panel to the primary crossbar, pull the first cord at the left down inside the again of the crossbar, then up in the the front and down within the returned of once more, as established in photograph below. Pull the free quit tightly downward.

1. pull cord
down behind
crossbar

2. bring cord
up in front of
cross bar,
then drop
down behind

3. pull
downward
tightly.

Now take the following cord and fix it to the crossbar inside the same fashion, besides alternating the commands. This time you will begin with it inside the front of crossbar, then pull up in the back of it, then down within the front; tighten. the subsequent (3rd) twine will pass in the back of the bar similar to the primary one, and the fourth wire will begin in the the front like the 1/3.

Pull the 4 dangling ends firmly; tie a square Knot immediately beneath the wood crossbar.

Still keep on draping the cords inside the alternating fashion over the crossbar. Then make firm rectangular Knots with every employer of four cords. See image below.

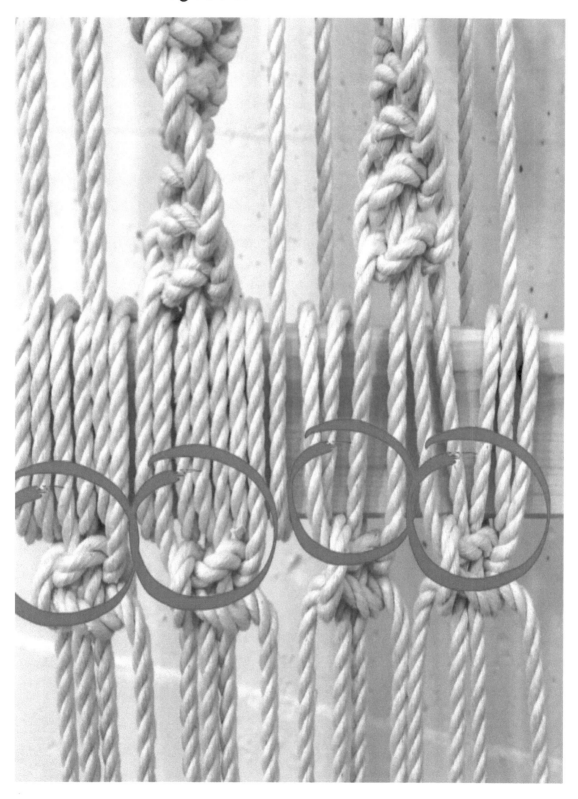

This is what the finished top panel need to look like:

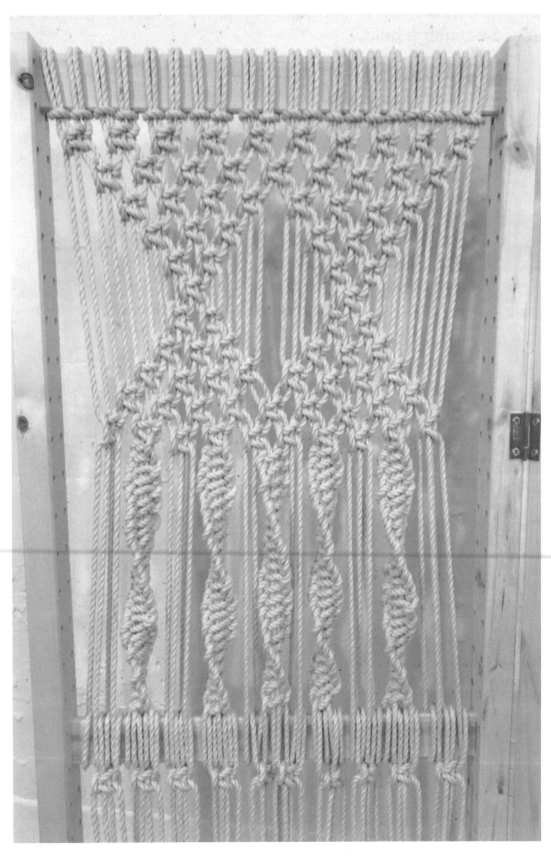

Step 6: In the middle segment

You currently have the pinnacle section of the panel finished and a row of rectangular Knots simply beneath the crossbar.

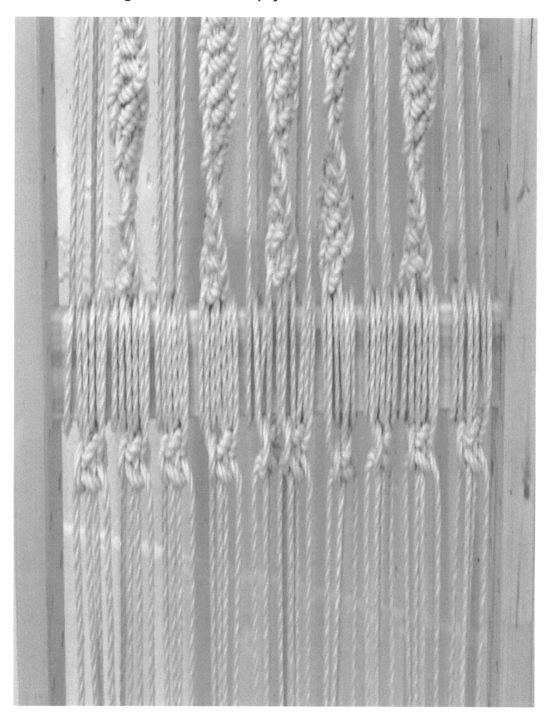

Right now below this row, weave the subsequent collection:

• beginning with the third character wire from the left, tie a rectangular Knot. Then tie any other square Knot right away below the primary knot.

• pass the subsequent four character cords.

• Tie another rectangular Knot (with a second knot without delay underneath it.)

• pass 4 greater cords.

• Tie every other square Knot (with a second knot directly beneath it.)

• skip four extra cords.

• Tie every other square Knot (with a second knot at once under it.)

• skip 4 more cords.

• Tie a totally closing rectangular Knot (with a 2d knot without delay beneath it.)

• pass the remaining 2 man or woman cords.

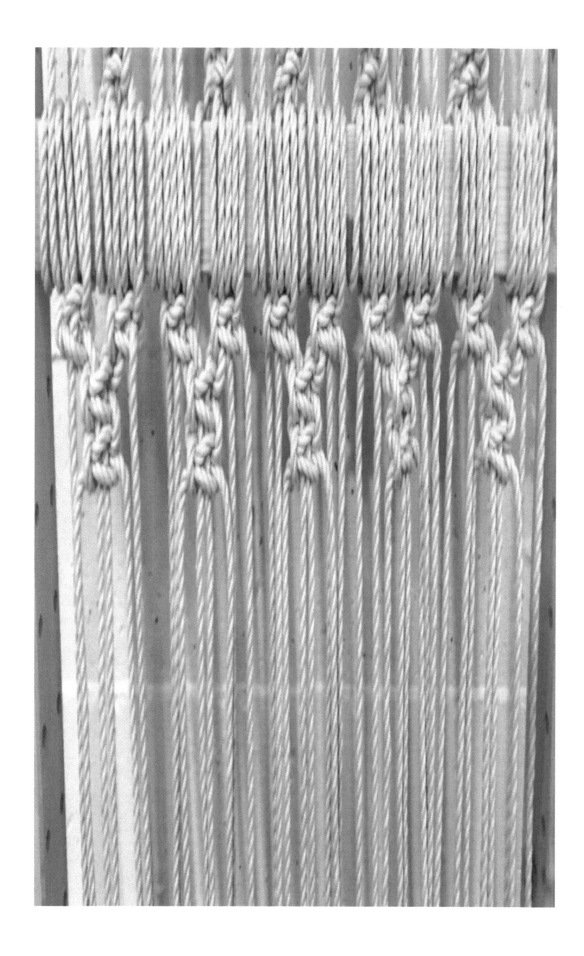

In order to complete this center phase, comply with the collection beneath:

- Continuing with the 7th person twine from the left, about four" above the pinnacle of the second one wood crossbar, tie a rectangular Knot. Then tie a 2d square Knot at once beneath it.

- pass the subsequent 4 character cords.

- 4" above the crossbar, tie a square Knot (with a second knot at once under it.)

- bypass four cords.

- Four" above the crossbar, tie a square Knot (with a 2d knot right now below it.)

- bypass 4 cords.

- Four" above the crossbar, and tie a square Knot (with a 2nd knot at once underneath it.)

- pass the ultimate 6 person cords.

2 stacked
Square Knots

4"

4"

Now, starting with the 1st cord at the left, make a row across of rectangular Knots. They should fall right above the top of the crossbar.

To cozy the center panel to the second crossbar, separate the free cords (with 1st & third cords in the back of and 2nd & 4th cords inside the the front), as show in picture underneath. Then, without delay under the crossbar, the usage of the ones 4 loose cords, tie a comfy rectangular Knot. do this during for all of the cords.

Step 7: – bottom section

You're nearly achieved with this complete panel! only some more steps.

- beneath the final row of rectangular Knots, staring with the seventh person twine, tie a rectangular Knot, bypass 4 cords, square Knot, pass 4, square Knot, bypass 4, square Knot, skip 6

- starting with the 3rd cord from left, tie a 1/2 of rectangular Spiral Knot till it is 7" lengthy

- keep tying half rectangular Spiral Knots (7" long) in among every of the rectangular Knots from the preceding row

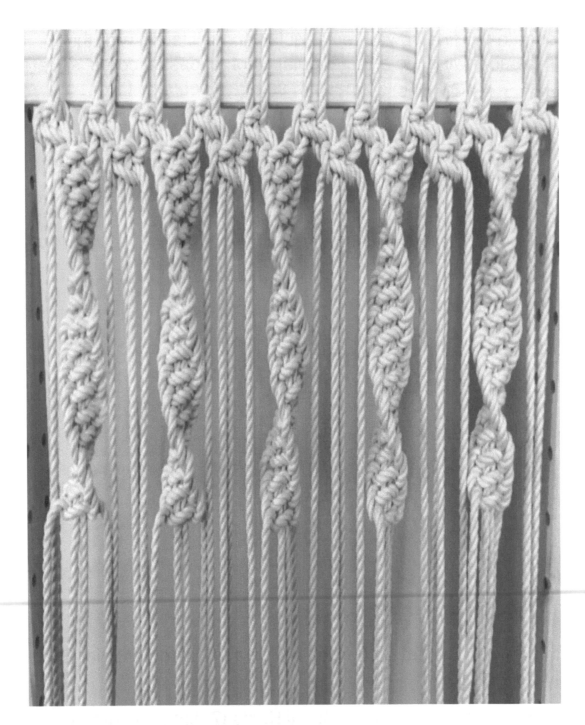

•   Make several random knots within the unfastened cords, as proven below, truly to add a few texture.

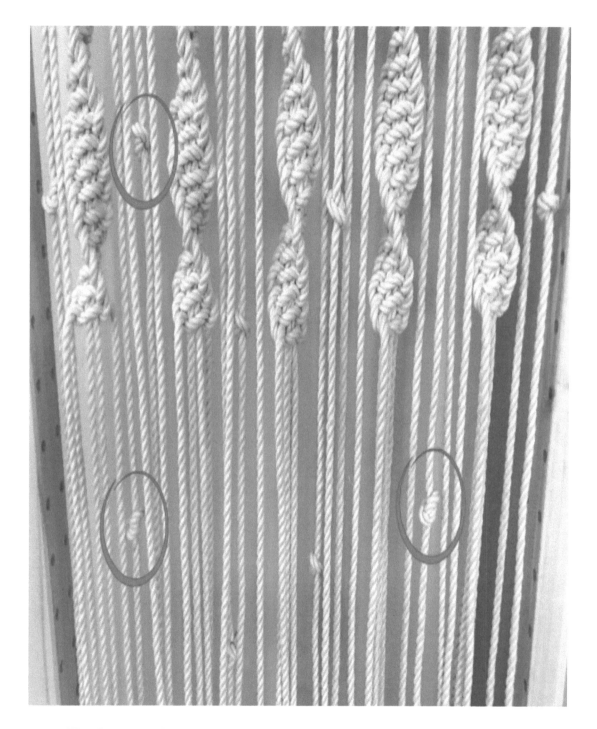

- Tie knots close to the lowest of each cord, slightly staggered at numerous heights, then fray the ends. This lends a piece of Bohemian taste to the design.

Step 8: clothing backing

Lining the once more of the wooden display body with material is completely non-compulsory. If the usage of the show display to hide a closet or garage place, but, it's best to preserve the mess hidden from view! If you decide to line the again, there are also a ton of fabric alternatives.

I decided to go with a simple white muslin material; it's less expensive and creates a gentle historical past for the sculptural experience of the macramé design. The use of a stapler gun, I linked the fabric to the again of the timber body.

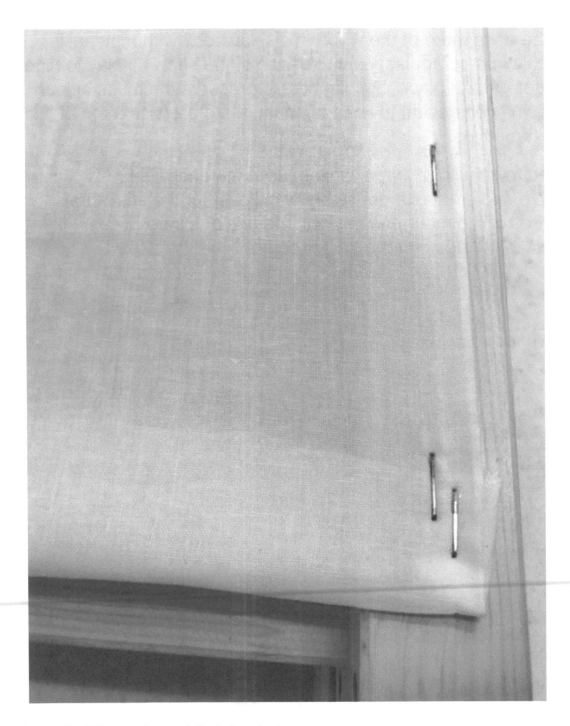

Step 9: Wow almost finished step

That's right. You're nearly there! just repeat steps 1 via 8 for the very last frames. Now just issue once more and admire your work! I promise your friends will envy this macrame folding show display screen.

Fantastic projects look above; trust you enjoy making this fantastic
macramé hanging room divider making project? Thanks for following

the steps just try making another project yourself.